輕

觸瞬間

Touch 닿음 梁世恩 Zipcy 著

中文版序

一開始的動機，是憐愛。

某天，我看著睡著的戀人，內心升起了滿滿愛憐的情緒。
於是我悄悄的躺在他身邊，靜靜的擁抱他，
感到非常溫暖與幸福。

那感覺，不只是肌膚與肌膚的相觸，而是超越了身體的真實感與親密感。

真是神奇呢。
只要彼此有愛，即便只是一個眼神的交會，心就會波濤洶湧；
即便只是觸碰到指尖，心也能怦然而動。

還有更加神奇的喔，
在韓國的我所創作的畫，居然能在異國他處，與各位見面。

希望這本書的溫度，能好好傳達到你心中，
成為你溫暖的撫觸，柔和的慰藉。

Zipcy

Part 1

His story and Her story

他和她的故事，開始了

Part 2

Love is touch

愛，就是每天都渴望觸碰你的心

前言
Prologue

輕觸，瞬間。

肌膚與肌膚的相觸，
雖然只是純粹的、物理性的觸碰，
但在那一剎那，心臟會如同跳電般猛烈震動，
那感覺，彷彿飄浮在雲朵上，像血液都倒流，也像在溫暖的水中悠遊。
於是我將那些千滋百味，百感交集的神祕瞬間，一一畫了下來。

Touch

Flesh on flesh.
It may only be brief: a graze, or light contact.
But in that split second, it is infinitely more: it clenches your heart,
it takes you above the clouds, it causes a blood rush, it floats you on calm waters.
These illustrations depict that moment of mysterious sensations and a million thoughts.

Part 1

His story and Her story

他和她的故事，開始了

第一次，四目相對

The Beginning

他的故事

我還記得，她的視線在空中流轉，我們第一次四目交接。
雖然只有一剎那，卻強烈地襲擊了我的瞳孔，
過了好幾天也難以忘卻。

his story

I remember when your wondering gaze landed on me for the first time.
It was momentary, but the image of you became vividly etched
on my mind, and lingered for many days after.

她的故事

即使看向別處，也能感受到他不容忽視的炙熱視線，
彷彿在呼喚著我，
轉頭望去，在烏黑髮絲之間，
一道閃亮的強光向我襲來。

心臟怦——地，猛然一跳。

her story

I felt your eyes on me, though I was faced away.
They were calling for me, so I turned around to answer.
Between the curtain of black hair, your gaze was aimed at me,
and I felt my heart drop.

他的故事

從我面前經過的女孩，身上散發著
如4月飄落的紫丁香花瓣般的淡紫色香味，
一起暫時靜止，又突然消散，
忽然之間，
我好想埋進她的胸口，
沉浸於她的香氣之中。

his story

She brushed by, and in the space she had occupied seconds previously,
was a smell of lilacs and April, lavender in color and fleeting.
And I had a thought…
Oh how I would love to keep that scent resting on her chest with me.

她的故事

就像在充滿陽光的午後，將頭舒服的埋入枕頭，
就像感受著衣服纖維裡，你的香氣與柔軟的觸感混在一起，
彷彿只要臉頰埋進那香味中，我就會安心的，慵懶欲睡。
突然好想，緊緊抱住他。

her story

It's like burying your face in an afternoon pillow filled with sunshine,
it's like that feeling of comfort from smells and the feel of skin and fresh laundry.
It's enough to put me right to a state of comfort, seizing me with a sudden thought of him, and of holding him.

她的故事

第一次握住他的手之前，
我來回輕輕摩挲著他的手指——
心臟啊，為什麼跳得那麼劇烈呢？

her story

It was the first time we held hands.
In that moment when his fingers found mine, and slid in between,
I felt a million butterflies in my stomach.

他的故事

那一晚，
我與她第一次十指相扣。
那瞬間，就像拼上了最後一片拼圖，
我的全身，升起一股顫慄。

his story

That night,
when her hands filled every crevice of mine,
there was a sense of completion.
Completion, like the last piece of a puzzle had been found, and fit in its rightful place.

髮絲間，游移的手

Comb My Hair

他的故事

她纖細美麗的指尖
在我的髮絲之間上下游移、探索，

我彷彿能從髮稍感覺到她輕柔的撫摸，
一次又一次。

his story

When her dainty fingers comb my hair in a slow and steady motion,
each strand of my hair feels revived, alive.

她的故事

當他的指尖撫觸我的髮，
心頭頓時湧上一陣酥麻。

掠過髮絲的指尖，傳來了微妙的顫動，
彷彿在悄悄對我訴說：
我想更了解妳，想觸及、深入妳的心。

her story

His uncertain fingers graze my hair, sending my heart racing.
A very slight tremor courses through his fingertips,
and whispers to me, "I want to get to know you better, I want to feel you more."

你的臉龐
Your Cheeks

他的故事

妳的臉頰怎麼會如此柔軟呢，
好想將妳那無與倫比的肌膚觸感
隨身攜帶。
這是我最大的願望。

his story

I'm in awe of the softness of your skin.
If only I could have this softness for good.

她的故事

摸起來有些粗糙，略略單薄，

怎麼會這樣，比起我柔嫩的皮膚，
你的觸感更好。

her story

Slightly dry to the touch, lightly translucent to the eyes,
I would rather have my hands on your skin than mine.

他的故事

不想錯過妳緊貼在我耳旁，那細柔的呼吸，
我將所有感官都集中在耳朵。

妳的一呼一吸如此甜蜜，令我一陣迷茫。

his story

All my senses were focused on my ears, so that I may not miss the sound of your breath.
On a particularly sharp gasp,
I felt my mind was lost, lost in an abyss.

她的故事

伴隨你低沉的嗓音，
你的嘴脣若有似無的輕碰著我的耳朵，
比想像得更加柔軟。

因為你嘴脣傳來的熱氣，
因為我耳朵升起的溫度，
彼此相觸之處，漸漸燒得通紅。

her story

The gentle murmur of his low voice filling my head,
his soft lips lightly brushing against my ear.
Maybe it was his lips, or maybe it was the heat,
but I felt hot and feverish wherever his hands landed.

她的故事

雨的氣味，亞麻的觸感，你的體溫
還有與雨聲交纏的，你的聲音。

her story

The smell of the rain, the feel of the linen,
the heat of your body.
The sound of your breathing between the gentle plop,
plop of the rain.

他的故事

在雨聲之中，交雜著妳細柔的呼吸聲，
那是比這世上任何音樂，都更和諧優美的唱和。

his story

The harmony between the sound of your delicate breaths
and the raindrops is the greatest symphony.

他的故事

從頸項一路延伸到背部的曲線，
在妳被汗水浸濕的短髮之間
藏著那顆只有我才知道的、小小的痣——

好美，
美得足以攫住我的呼吸與視線。

his story

The curve flowing from your neck to your back,
the tiny, secret little mole covered by your sweaty hair…
Your every detail takes my breath away.

她的故事

你靜靜靠近，
輕輕埋在我脖頸間，來回摩挲，
真像一隻可愛的拉布拉多。

her story

You are beyond adorable,
when you come to me and gently nuzzle your head between my neck and shoulder.

你的手臂
Your Arms

他的故事

她纖細修長的手指
從我的手肘，沿著手臂緩緩向上滑，
肩膀傳來屬於她的熱氣，
讓我一時忘記了呼吸。

「妳的撫摸，好像喚醒了我未知的感官呢。」

his story

Your thin fingertips climb all the way up my arm,
between my elbow and shoulder, they escalate and descend,
making me forget how to breathe.
Your touch wakes up the deepest parts of me that I had not known of.

她的故事

緊緊抱住你厚實的臂膀，
實在好溫暖，充滿安全感，

現在，也好想緊緊攬住你的手臂。

her story

Your warm and strong arms,
linked with mine and held to my chest⋯.
They fill me with thoughts of being entirely wrapped in their warm embrace.

他的故事

悶熱的夏季來到尾聲，
夜晚不知何時開始變涼了。

伴隨昆蟲的鳴唱，
冰涼啤酒襯著妳熾熱的體溫，
讓今夜的心情好得開始微醺起來。

his story

The end of a sweltering summer
A cool night breeze, singing insects in the distance
The warmth of your skin on mine
And the chill of a cold beer—
An evening of blissful intoxication

他的故事

順著妳的腰線淡淡滑過的剪影，
突顯出這世界上
最完美的曲線。

his story

My eyes follow the line that
descends toward your waist.
To the silhouette
that forms a perfect,
flawless curve.

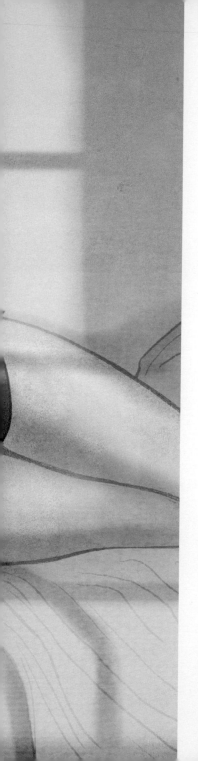

她的故事

我感受到你的視線，
從我的肩膀緩緩往下流瀉，
慢慢的，在腰間盤旋。
即使未用手碰觸，我也感到一陣麻癢，
還有一些些，微妙的緊張。

her story

Your gaze traces my outline
to linger on the curve of my waist,
making my skin quiver,
my heart flutter.

他的故事

即使窄小纖瘦，
卻能默默撫慰我疲憊心靈的──
妳溫暖的肩膀。

his story

Refuge is found, peace is discovered
An all-accepting silence
In the warmth of your small, narrow shoulders.

她的故事

比起萬語千言，
我更能從你寬闊靜謐的肩膀裡，
得到厚實的安全感。

her story

Comfort is found, relief is discovered
More meaningful than a thousand words
In the expanse of your broad,
steady shoulders.

她的故事

當被他深深攬入懷中，
熾熱的體溫襲來——

我瞬間感到一陣暈眩。

her story

An excited quiver, a surprised gasp escaped me,
when your arms encircled my waist,
and your warmth enveloped me.

他的故事

好想保護她，
又怕嚇到她，
遲疑了好久，終於將她攬入懷中，
我感受到弱小的她，正微微顫抖。

his story

Prolonged hesitation,
of whether I should extend my arm;
I felt a soft tremor,
when my arm cradled your waist.

仔細盯著你的臉，
怎麼會那麼可愛呢……
我悄悄地想。

When I look at you,
I wonder,
How are you so lovely?

她的故事

你的體溫從背後傳來，一陣暖洋洋的，
彷彿明天的煩惱都被熱度融化，煙消雲散了。

his story

Against my back,
you exude the warmth that
melts tomorrow's troubles.

背後的重量
The Weight Against My Back

她的故事

雖然我被你緊緊抱著，卻更像是我在擁抱著你。
你靜靜靠在我背後，身體的重量一點一點傳來，

今天的你，好像不太開心呢。

her story

It's me in your arms, but it's you in my embrace too;
the weight of you against my back is unusually sad today.

就像白天與夜晚的溫度差，
你的溫度越來越炙熱。

Your body feels ever warmer as the nights get colder.

溫差 2
Time of the Year
of Warm Days and Chilly Evenings

「你的身體好燙，
好像超過36.5度，快要38度了。」

「因為這種天氣，妳的手總是很冰，
我要分享溫暖給妳啊。」

"It feels as though
your body temperature is
set to 38, not 36.5."

"Perhaps
that is so I can share a few degrees of warmth with you,
on a shivery night like this."

她的故事

好神奇喔，
只要將頭靠在你的膝蓋上，
沉甸甸的腦袋，
就會變得很放鬆。

her story

How strange it is that my head
should feel so much lighter and clearer,
resting on your knees.

膝蓋
Knees
2

她的故事

他小心翼翼的，為我的傷口塗藥膏，
輕柔的指尖碰觸著我的膝蓋，
一股怦然的電流，瞬間竄入心底。

肌膚被撫觸著，麻麻癢癢的，
疼痛什麼的，早就忘得乾乾淨淨了。

her story

Gently, you apply ointment
to a little wound on my knee.

The tremor of your fingertips
stir something inside,
making the sense of thrill harder to ignore than
the stinging on my knee.

紅葉與晚霞，
還有我對你的心意，
在這被鮮豔橘紅色渲染的季節裡。

A season when autumn leaves,
fall sunsets and my unwavering feelings for you
all cascade into hues of brilliant orange.

他的故事

睡著的妳，真可愛。

微張的嘴唇輕吐著氣息，
臉頰陷入枕頭裡，在夢中微微皺著眉。

一切都太可愛了，我就這麼欣賞著，
直到睡著。

his story

How enchanting you are, asleep.
The rhythm of your breath between your parted lips,
your cheeks pressed against the pillow,
the crinkle of your forehead.
Everything is so lovable, my eyes linger a while
before I fade away to sleep.

她的故事

睡著的你，真可愛。
用指尖仔細確認你的眼睫毛，一根一根，
順著眉毛的線條輕輕劃過，
再滑向你微微顫動的嘴脣⋯⋯

一切都太可愛了，
讓我一直偷偷撫摸著，停不下來。

her story

How enchanting you are, asleep.
The feel of each flutter of your eyelashes,
the crease of your brows at my touch,
the purse of your lips.
Everything is so sweet, my fingers long to linger.

他的故事

我將臉埋入妳的頸間，
聆聽妳的脈搏輕輕跳動的聲音，
妳幽微的體香傳來，使我的鼻尖騷動，
身體也漸漸變得慵懶。

his story

The reason I nuzzle at your neck.

I am at total peace,
by the warmth of your heat shrouding my face,
the gentle thump of your heart beating,
and the subtle,

nose-tickling smell of your skin.

她的故事

在即使戴上手套，手指還是很冰冷的日子，
我的手卻能在你的頸間融化。
即使突然的冰冷會使你嚇一跳，
你卻從不拒絕，
用頸項的溫度包容我，
你的心意，比頸間的炙熱更溫暖，
也在無形中，緊緊擁抱我。

her story

On an early winter day
a little too soon for gloves,
my cold fingers find warmth along your neck.
You must have been surprised by the sudden chill,
but you let me nestle my hands there...
Keeping me warm,
not just with your body heat,
but with your kindness.

「我們的愛，還有多久保存期限？」

偶爾會這樣沒來由的不安，
打從心底害怕起來……

Sometimes I sit and wonder if
you and I have an expiration date.
And such silly ponderings leave my heart aching,

他的故事

躺在她的膝頭，像個孩子般倚靠她，
她會專注、輕柔地撫摸我的耳朵，
我很享受那微小平凡的一刻。

對我來說，那是很陌生的感覺，
也有點擔心會不會痛，
但當我把自己完全交付給她，看到她溫柔的笑容，
我感到滿滿的幸福。

his story

I gave myself to her,
as a child would to his mother.
She cleared a very personal part of me,
and was pleased to do so.

It was something new,
and I worried it might hurt;
but the moment I put myself at her mercy,
and saw her give such a genuine smile,
I felt happiness—sheer, sincere happiness.

她的故事

你突然說，想要幫我修指甲，
雖然不明所以，卻感到自己被寵愛著。

你用寬大厚實的手，輕柔的幫我修剪著，
好像變得比平時更穩重，
更令人心跳加速了。

her story

Asking to file my nails was a quirky request,
but one that made me feel loved.

I won't deny the flutter of butterflies in my stomach
as your large hands so gently,
warmly caressed my own.

他的故事

我的指尖還殘留橘子冰涼的觸感，
又碰到妳溫熱的嘴脣——

那感受……該怎麼形容才好呢？

his story

No single word can sufficiently describe
the sensation I feel at the tips of my fingers
when coolness of the clementine pieces
overlap with the warmth of your lips.

她的故事

你潔淨的肌膚上還殘留著水珠，
細細的睫毛與黝黑的頭髮，
帶有微微的濕氣，
最喜歡你這個模樣了。

her story

When I see droplets of water on your clear, gleaming skin,
When I see your long lashes and dark hair still glistening,
I adore how you look.

Part 2

Love is touch

愛，就是每天都渴望觸碰你的心

是這世界上最安穩的所在。

Your embrace—the serenest,
most comforting space of all.

她的故事

愛，真能如此熾烈嗎？
曾有那麼一刻，心中閃過這種想法。

當你說：「好想看清楚妳的臉。」
你輕輕將我的髮絲撥到耳後，連指尖都滿是情意；
當你用灼熱的眼神，彷彿要將我看穿時⋯⋯

只要你的一個動作，一個眼神，
那些熾熱的瞬間，讓我彷彿置身於溫暖的水域。

her story

There comes a time when you wonder,
was the feeling of being loved this tender?

Like that moment when you whispered,
"Let me see more of your face,"
and tucked my hair gently behind my ear,
or that moment when your little gestures
and brief glances bathed me in a warm and soothing glow.

她的故事

你的臉逐漸靠近，彷彿快要吻上我的脣，
我輕輕閉上雙眼，卻感到鼻尖被輕輕一啄。

你慵懶的看著我問：
「妳知道親吻鼻尖有什麼涵義嗎？」
「什麼？」
「代表妳很珍貴。」

你的微笑，和那美好的答案，至今仍鮮活得宛如昨日。

her story

I cast down my eyes when you brought your face close as if to kiss me.
Instead, you gave me a peck on my nose.
And holding my gaze, you asked,
"Do you know what a kiss on the nose means?"
"Hmm?"
"It means to me, you are so dear."
That moment of such a sweet answer, of such a tender smile,
is on an infinite loop in my head.

他的故事

與嘴唇相觸時的感覺有些不同，
鼻翼之間隱藏著羞澀的溫柔，
朦朧卻堅定的，傳遞過來。

Like a kiss, not like a kiss—

Feeling the soft tempo of your affection converging on the tip of your nose.

她的故事

喜歡將身體完全的緊靠著你，
偶爾會想像，要是能像磁鐵那樣貼在一起該有多好，
也有點擔心你會討厭這樣的我⋯⋯

「如果太重我就下來。」我擔心的説。
「妳別動。」

最喜歡你的溫柔了。

her story

This closeness makes me happy,
and I sometimes wish you'd be glued to me.

But worried you might be annoyed, I say,
"I'll get off if I'm too heavy."

…I love the warmth with which you softly reply,
"It's ok. Stay."

他的故事

有時，好想聽聽妳的心跳聲，
將臉埋進妳胸前，貼上耳朵，
當聲音逐漸變得鮮明，耳邊感受到細微的跳動，
還有在我懷中，柔軟的妳。

這一切，最讓我感到安心。

his story

Some days I just want to lie and listen to the sound of your heartbeat.
I place my ear close to your chest and close my eyes;
and the gentle thumps grow steadily louder,
the pulses cause your chest to bump against my ear,
and your arms couldn't feel any softer…
All of the sensations blend together and I'm put in a trance-like daydream.

他的故事

我換衣服時，她最喜歡跑來搔我癢，看我驚訝的表情。
當我的肌肉因她的指尖滑過而緊繃，
「哎唷，你要放鬆才好玩啊。」
埋怨的眼神，不滿意的嘴角，有些傲嬌的微笑……
妳真是有夠可愛。

his story

Catching sight of me changing, she would scurry over to tickle me, searching my face for my reaction.

Listening as she whispered, with a mischievous look and a smirk,
"I like you squishy,"
I would tense where her hands grazed me... ending in a heart in a wild overdrive.

她的故事

趁他脫掉了衣服，我跑去搔弄他光裸的身體。
最喜歡用手指感受他柔軟溫暖的皮膚，
悄悄用手掌丈量他寬闊的胸膛。
他的腹肌隱隱用力，一粒粒雞皮疙瘩豎起，
實在太可愛了，總讓我忍不住笑出來。

her story

Catching sight of him undressing, I would always patter over to tickle him.

I adored running my fingertips against his silky, warm skin,
And wondering about the number of hands it would take to cover all of him.

I couldn't stifle a giggle as I watched him tuck in and flex his stomach,
And as little goosebumps spread across his skin.

「哎呀，討厭。」

Naughty boy.

結束疲憊的一天，
開一罐啤酒，
在這樣的夜晚，
分享彼此瑣碎的生活。

午餐吃了什麼？今天有什麼事嗎？
你總是問我同樣的問題，
關心我那單調乏味的日常。

一股感謝油然而生的
這樣的夜晚。

A night,
sharing the small details
of the day
over a can of beer.

What did you have for lunch?
Anything out of the ordinary?

A night,
where your small interest
in my daily affairs
makes me so grateful.

…Where a pat on the back
is the perfect end to the day.

這季節，空氣中溫柔彌漫。

在櫻花盛開的樹下，
連呼吸都覺得很甜。

A season of tender breezes.
Even the air itself is sweet,
underneath the petals of cherry blossoms dancing in the wind.

這季節，空氣中溫柔彌漫 2
A Season of Tender Breezes

每年都會盛開的花瓣，依然令人心動，
每年都能欣賞的風景，還是感覺新鮮。

每一年，從你天真無邪的臉龐上看見
春天綻放的剎那——
迷人依舊的你。

The same flowers,
yet they always tug at my heart.
The same scenery,
yet somehow it always feels different.

The same you, but all you do feels fresh and new…
Even the sight of you trying to preserve a fleeting moment.

A new spring; the same lovely you.

我偶爾能這樣，從高處俯瞰你——

喜歡這樣從上方看著你的那些時刻：
溫柔的為我綁好鞋帶，
或是總站在低一個階梯處，深情擁抱我。

Sometimes, when I'm standing above you—

I like where you are, beneath my gaze.

Especially when,
You tie up my loose shoelaces,
Or embrace me from a step below.

總是必須抬頭才能仰望的你，
當你仰頭看我，那眼神，那面容，
不知怎地，比平時更教人愛憐。

You are most times above my gaze,
So when I see your eyes looking up at me,

I find you beyond adorable.

她的故事

最喜歡撫摸你的耳垂了。
軟軟的，嫩嫩的，
彷彿嬰兒的肌膚般，
好喜歡。

her story

The soft, fleshy feel of your earlobes
reminds me of a baby's delicate, velvety skin—
Making them one of my favorite parts of you.

如陽光般，和煦溫暖的你。

Someone as warm as the rays of the sun.

請你撫慰我
Place Your Hands on Me

他的故事

妳看我的眼神，彷彿在低語著──「我愛你」，
一次又一次的撫觸，洋溢著妳滿滿的珍愛。

「幹嘛這麼深情的看著我？」
「因為很幸福啊。」

his story

Your gaze whispers, "I love you,"
while your hands caressing me murmur, "you are dear to me."

"Why are you looking at me like that?"
"Because I am happy."

額頭
Forehead

她的故事

睡著前，
在我額頭印上輕輕一吻吧。

只要這一個小小舉動，
就能感受到巨大的愛。

her story

Just a peck on my forehead please,
before we fall asleep.

Because, although it's a small gesture,
it makes me feel incredibly loved.

拍拍──
沒事了，一切都會好的。

「只要你在我身邊，一切都會好起來。」

Comfort.

"Don't worry, everything will be all right."
"With you by my side, I feel like things will work themselves out."

緊緊抱住你，
就能聽見你心跳的聲音，怦怦，怦怦……

緊緊貼住彼此的胸口，
心跳的節奏也逐漸同步，
就好像我和你，開始共度的每一分、每一秒。

所謂的擁抱，
就是將彼此的心跳與時間，
合而為一。

When I wrap you in my embrace,
I can feel your heart beat against mine.

When their rhythms start to perfectly align,
it's like the timelines of your life and mine converge,

Being in each other's arms is the act of two hearts becoming one, two timelines becoming one.

「對不起。」
他的聲線
充滿焦急的熱度，
使我冰凍的心，開始融化。

"I'm sorry."
His quiet voice
and apologetic warmth
free my wounded heart.

這樣犯規啦。

This apology is no fair.

點綴季節的，燦爛之花。

A flower
weaving the boundaries
between seasons.

這一刻，你讓我明白，
我是這世界上最重要的存在。

In this moment,

If you want to tell me
You value me most in the world,

無須任何言語，
只要我手背上那輕輕的一吻，
便已足夠。

You need not say anything,
Just give me a kiss on my hand.

Because that's all I need.

輕觸・瞬間
Touch

在無意識中，
我們的身軀逐漸交纏，
卻一點也不難過，
反而感到更溫暖、更安心。

因為你對我而言，是如此特別。

突然從夢中醒來，感受到你的體溫，
一切都那麼自然，如此熟悉，
啊，我的小確幸。

To have you there next to me
Tousle-haired and half awake...

You feel warm, so soft,
And there is no sense of discomfort—

And to know it's you,
Of all people...

I can call it happiness, at its most genuine,
To have you there, so familiar,
Just as I'm rising from sleep.

我的雙腳，融化在你掌心

Your Sweet Touch, That Warms My Feet

「妳的腳好冰喔，看來天氣真的變冷了呢。」
我的雙腳總是最先感受到季節的溫差變化，
你毫不猶豫的，
伸出厚實的雙手摩挲起我的雙腳⋯⋯
真喜歡你，好謝謝你。
我心裡偷偷想著，怎麼會有這麼溫柔的人呢。

一點都不美的我的雙腳，被你牢牢握在手心，
害羞之餘，
卻也融化在你直截了當的體貼與熱度裡。

忍不住想，即使過了很久很久以後，
當這樣的季節來臨，
你還是會像現在一樣為我取暖吧，
讓我不用再穿襪子了。
不過，你會有點辛苦呢。

I know colder weather is coming when your feet need warming up...
My feet react first to the dropping of temperatures,
and when I see you wrapping your large hands around my feet,
caressing them, warming them,
I wonder how a person can be so sweet.

At the same time,
I feel a bit shy about placing my rough and battered feet in your hands,
but maybe that's how I can feel closer to you.

And I think to myself,
After years have passed and yet another winter is upon us,
I hope you will be here, hands cupping my feet.
Even if it's a bit more work
than passing me a pair of socks.

下雨的日子，
和你一起喝一杯，滋味特別甘甜。

你的嗓音跟雨聲相互交融，
甜蜜極了。

On this rainy evening,
the drink I sip with you is sweeter than any other.

凌晨的香氣
Dawn

我很喜歡凌晨時分，
世界一片靜謐，空氣也被染成靛藍色，

我沉醉的撫摸著你，
與你在午夜之中相擁。
多麼美妙的時刻。

Dawn.

I love…
the scent of a neighborhood waking from a night of slumber,
and the intoxicating feel of you, warm in this chill of the break of dawn.

早晨，一睜開眼睛
When I Open My Eyes

他的故事

睜開眼，第一個映入眼簾的是妳，
這是多麼令人感動的早晨。

妳的秀髮蓬亂散開，
眼睛和臉頰也有些浮腫，
但就連淺淺的鼻息，也那麼可愛。

使我不自覺揚起嘴角，看得入迷。

his story

In the first rays of the morning, when I open my eyes, I see you;
the tangled hair, the ever-so-slightly puffy cheeks and eyes, the steady breathing.
It's so endearing, I lay and watch for a while... Thankful to start my day off with a smile.

她的故事

睜開眼，第一個映入眼簾的是你，
這是多麼令人感動的早晨。

你毫無防備的表情，
如孩子般單純可愛，
讓我忍不住想不停親吻你的臉。

her story

Thankful that you're the first thing I see when I wake up in the morning.

You look so unguarded, so innocent,
I want to kiss you and kiss you again all over your cheeks.

"Good morning."
我的一天，從你愛憐的嗓音開始。

"Good morning,"
Starting my day with the sweet sound of your voice.

湛藍的空氣。

Cobalt blue air.

她的故事

雖然也喜歡在這樣的節日裡，
一起走在響起聖誕歌的街道上，來一場浪漫約會，

但我更喜歡
與你一起縮進溫暖的電熱毯，
你溫柔的剝橘子餵我吃，
我懶懶地躺在你懷中。

her story

A stroll along the decorated,
carol-filled streets would be delightful,
but I would still rather be nestled in my warm blankets with you,
idling the afternoon away snacking on the clementine pieces
you put in my mouth.

最喜歡的魔幻時刻
Our Most Favorite Time

與你一起欣賞晚霞瞬息萬變的時刻。

Our most favorite time
Sunset with you.

她的故事

秋日的天空如此美麗，
好喜歡映入我瞳孔中的，
你的側臉，
以及那閃閃發光的眼睛。

her story

I'm enamored
with the sight of you looking out and breathing in the gorgeous fall sky,
with eyes reflecting the brilliant colors.

日落時分的漫步
Sunset

他的故事

在太陽逐漸落下的時刻，
與晚霞相互輝映的妳，如此動人。

his story

Sunset.
Strolls with you around dusk is my favorite time of the day.
Fading with the rays of the sun, you look so beautiful.

第一次,四脣相交的那一刻,
從你脣瓣傳來的那顫動、那溫度,是如此柔軟,
直到現在,所有感覺仍清晰地烙在心中。

Memories of the first kiss
Forever in my mind
is the feel of that first kiss:
the trembling, the heat,
the particular softness.

Part 3

Special page 01

從畫中，感受他們眼底蘊藏的愛憐

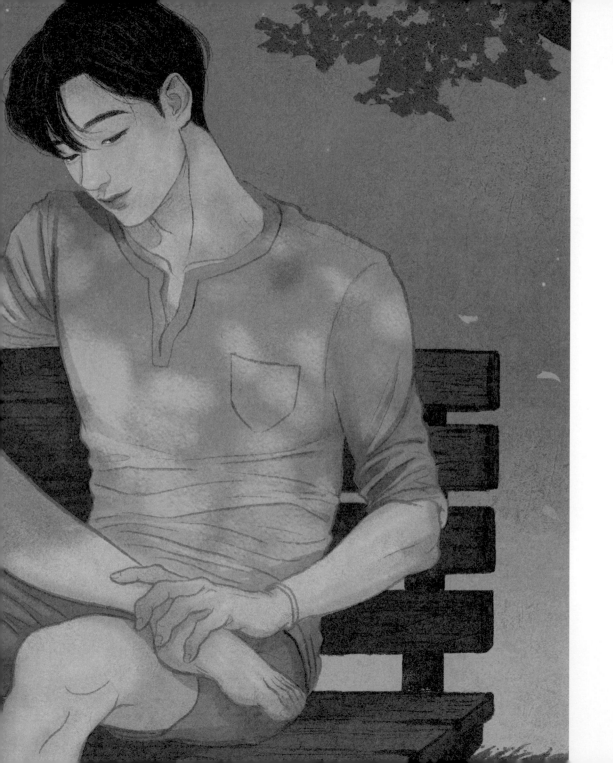

Part 4

Special page 02

Zipcy 創作過程解密

1. 先抓好框架與構圖，再大致畫出人物的輪廓。
2. 輪廓出來後，修正不滿意的部分，例如姿勢和臉的角度。
3. 接著，嘗試將整體構圖左右翻轉，比較看看，並確認有沒有疏漏的地方。
4. 男主角的鞋子穿了又脫、脫了又穿，脖子角度也修正了好幾遍，構圖才總算確定。
5. 確定好姿勢與整體構圖後，就可以開始畫細節了！
6. 在畫手腳的細節前，先標示出關節的地方，之後畫的時候會更輕鬆。
7. 這就是他與她的模樣誕生的過程。
8. 先約略畫出男主角的臉，再描繪肌肉線條，最後調整五官細節，就完成了。
9. 為了更突顯女主角溫柔的眼神，在眼睫毛的部分下了一番工夫。
10. 頭髮也要一絲一絲、細膩豐富的描繪出來。

11. 素描完成後，就可以進行上色了。
12. 先決定好基礎色調，再畫出明暗與亮點的地方。
13. 接著畫上背景。
14. 畫好陰影與粒子效果後，再次確認作品的整體調性。
15. 使用工具：觸控繪圖螢幕Cintiq Pro、PhotoshopCC。

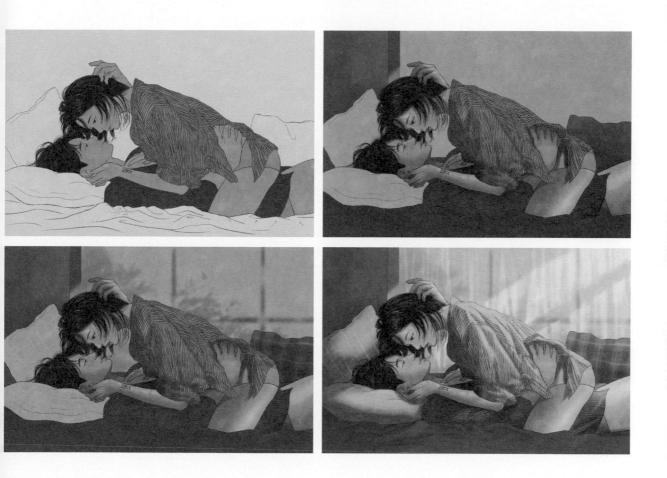

結語
Epilogue

從事插畫工作的9年後，我終於出版了首部單行本。起初接觸插畫時，我只是茫然的想著，只要持續做這件事做個10年，應該就能成就些什麼吧？就這樣忙碌的度過了這段時光。驀然回首，才發現當初隨意定下來的數字已經近在眼前了，這10年以來，我也一直調整自己的步伐，雖然緩慢，但我很快樂。

《輕觸瞬間Touch》這本書，是我在 Naver grafolio 的連載，集結了在這說長不長、說短不短的一年半之中的作品。起初收到連載邀請時，因為從來沒有嘗試過長期連載，其實很擔心自己能否勝任。

懶惰的我與其他多產的插畫家距離很遙遠，只憑藉著一個「親密接觸 skinship」的概念，就展開連載。連載期間，也一直很擔心自己能否在1年內畫出上百幅作品，創作素材是否足夠，以及要是畫風與內容太過重複，讀者會不會感到厭倦……種種的憂慮，讓我從連載開始前就生病了。

不過，人真的是很神奇，真的面對艱難的狀況時，反而會產生力量、想盡辦法去解決，雖然過程並不是一帆風順，但就結果來看，我也因為《輕觸瞬間Touch》得到了超乎預期的喜愛與關注。在許多支持與鼓勵下，我順利的完成了連載，也成長不少。

創作《輕觸瞬間Touch》的契機

這本書是描繪戀人肌膚相觸時、心動瞬間的故事。

相愛的人們在相互觸碰的那一秒，就能立刻感受從對方體溫傳來的舒暢與安穩感。當所愛之人度過了辛苦的一天、心情黯淡冰冷時，給他一個溫暖的擁抱，身體和心就能重新找回安全感，產生神祕的化學反應。

當我們想起一段逝去的關係，比起留戀早已遠離的那個人，其實更加懷念曾經愛過的日子、付出的感情與熱度。而在現在的感情中，最珍貴的也是彼此的感情和溫度。為了不要遺忘那些剎那，時時回想起當初的悸動，將它們好好珍藏，這就是我創作《輕觸瞬間Touch》的第一個目的。

我也發現，大多數作品要不是走天真爛漫的純情風，就是很成人的風格，有點兩極化。而我則希望遊走在感性（sensual）和性感（sexual）的分界線上，不一味追求刺激末梢神經的情慾或普遍級的安全地帶，而是以溫柔的方式，微妙的刺激著感官。因此我希望能畫出適合更多年齡層的作品，這是我的第二個目的。

關於畫作

我希望讀者在看到主角時，也能感受到那些「輕觸瞬間」，所以畫表情和動作時都經過一番苦思，努力想呈現出更生動的細節。因此，比起畫作風格，我更注重呈現畫裡想說的故事，結果很常被問是不是有真實人物作為創作的靈感來源。

畫主角的臉時，我喜歡想像自己平常喜歡的人物。人體也是先畫出骨架、在補上血肉、穿上衣服。其實我的解剖學沒有很好，大概是畫出來的感覺滿自然的，大家也都很捧場。

畫人體時如果真的遇上阻礙，我也會請老公充當模特兒幫忙，一起拍一張尷尬的照片做參考。意外的是，當我把夫妻一起拍的素材照上傳到社群網站後，居然引發熱烈迴響！甚至讓我開始考慮要不要一起放在書裡，不過最後考量到整體風格與色調而作罷。在這裡偷偷告訴想一探究竟的人：那些照片，我都有上傳到社群網站喔。

創作過程中，我花最多時間和精力的莫過於表現出「陷入愛河的眼神」。人的表情是很奧妙的，眼神是活靈活現或了無生氣，會根據瞳孔的位置角度、眼皮或睫毛形狀而不同。只要有一點點微小的差異，就可能會成為完全感受不到情感的創作。

因此當讀者告訴我，能感受到主角眼神中滿滿的愛時，我就知道自己費盡心力去傳達的情感，真的成功了！所以在我的創作裡，「眼神」一直是我最用心著墨的地方。

另一個也花費我許多心力的就是色調與構圖。畢竟在這本書中只有兩位主角，主題也設定為「親密接觸skinship」，並非具有連續情節的作品，必須避免太重複而顯得無聊。因此每一篇畫作，我都盡量避免使用類似姿勢，也不停變換色調。

雖然如此，仍難免會因為我的繪畫習慣，在無意識間畫出類似的作品，為了不讓讀者有「這不是以前畫過的嗎？怎麼又上傳了？」的感覺，所以後來我一直都有意識的進行各種嘗試和突破。

因此，可以看出在連載初期的畫和連載後期的作品有很大不同。雖然對我來說，我對所有作品都付出很多感情，無法區分優劣喜好，但這確實成為我獲得階段性成長的契機，是很有意義的挑戰。

除此之外，主角在親密觸碰彼此的構圖上，比起被動姿態，我更喜歡主動姿態。有的時候，我會讓女主角看起來更堅強、穩重，而男主角則顯得溫柔、弱小。我也會收集讀者提供的故事再做些許改編，對我來說，這些都是像禮物般珍貴的時光。

最後

很辛苦的一路走來，但也非常開心我終於做到了，可以無憾的畫下美好句點。即便依依不捨，但我會為了未來的「輕觸瞬間Touch」系列作品繼續充實自己、做好準備。

感謝一直都很相信我、支持我的盧昌洙社長；Grafolio的工作人員；為我出版第一本書、默默為我加油的朴善英社長；為了將英文翻譯得更具情感，給予很多幫助的adrienne。

更要感謝讀者朋友們，不停給予尚且不足的我滿滿的愛、幫助我達成這不可能的任務；還有每當我崩潰時，幫助我重新站起來的珍貴家人和朋友；以及永遠都給予我滿滿的愛和靈感的另一半。真的非常感謝與深愛著大家。

謝謝。

2018年秋
希望這本書能溫柔撫慰你的心
插畫家 Zipcy

「我愛你。」

輕觸瞬間Touch／梁世恩 Zipcy 著. YTING 譯. -- 初版. – 臺北市：時報文化，2020.11；面；19╳20公
分. --（FUN：76）

譯自：닿음

ISBN 978-957-13-8382-8（平裝）

1.戀愛 2.兩性關係

544.37　　　　　　　　　　　　　　　　　　　　　　　　　　　　　　　　　109014179

FUN 076

輕觸瞬間 Touch

닿음

作者 梁世恩 Zipcy｜**譯者** YTING｜**主編** 陳信宏｜**副主編** 尹蘊雯｜**執行企畫** 吳美瑤｜**美術協力** FE設計｜**編輯總監** 蘇清霖｜**董事長** 趙政岷｜**出版者** 時報文化出版企業股份有限公司　108019 臺北市和平西路三段240 號 3 樓　發行專線—(02)2306-6842　讀者服務專線—0800-231-705・(02)2304-7103　讀者服務傳真—(02)2304-6858　郵撥—19344724 時報文化出版公司　信箱—10899臺北華江橋郵局第99信箱　時報悅讀網—www.readingtimes.com.tw　電子郵件信箱—newlife@readingtimes.com.tw　時報出版愛讀者—www.facebook.com/readingtimes.2｜**法律顧問** 理律法律事務所　陳長文律師、李念祖律師｜**印刷** 和楹印刷有限公司｜**初版一刷** 2020年 11 月20日｜**定價** 新臺幣 450 元｜（缺頁或破損的書，請寄回更換）

時報文化出版公司成立於1975年，1999年股票上櫃公開發行，2008年脫離中時集團非屬旺中，以「尊重智慧與創意的文化事業」為信念。